Editor
Nancy Hoffman

Illustrator
Kevin McCarthy

Cover Artist
Brenda DiAntonis

Managing Editor
Karen J. Goldfluss, M.S. Ed.

Creative Director
Karen J. Goldfluss, M.S. Ed.

Art Production Manager
Kevin Barnes

Art Coordinator
Renée Christine Yates

Imaging
Rosa C. See
Ricardo Martinez
James Edward Grace

Publisher
Mary D. Smith, M.S. Ed.

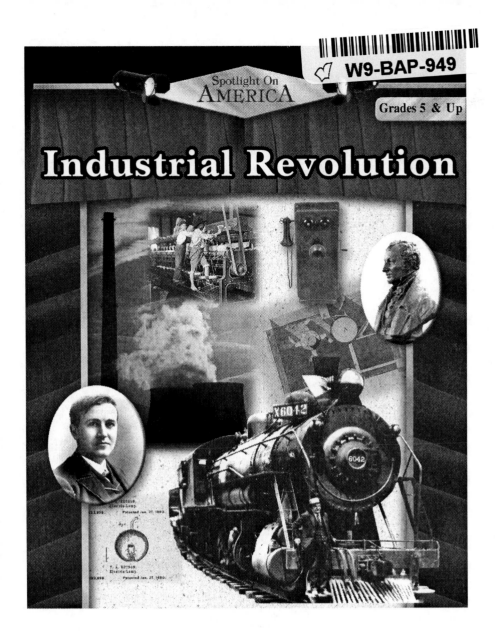

Spotlight On
AMERICA

Grades 5 & Up

Industrial Revolution

Author

Robert W. Smith

Teacher Created Resources, Inc.
6421 Industry Way
Westminster, CA 92683
www.teachercreated.com

ISBN: 978-1-4206-3220-0

© *2007 Teacher Created Resources, Inc.*
Reprinted, 2010
Made in U.S.A.

Teacher Created Resources

Table of Contents

Introduction 3

**Teacher Lesson Plans for
    Reading Comprehension**

The Industrial Revolution Begins 4

America's Industrial Revolution 4

Revolution in Transportation and
    Communication 5

The Gilded Age 5

Effects of the Industrial Revolution 6

Student Reading Pages

The Industrial Revolution Begins 7

America's Industrial Revolution 9

Revolution in Transportation and
    Communication 11

The Gilded Age 14

Effects of the Industrial Revolution 17

Reading Comprehension Quizzes

The Industrial Revolution Begins Quiz 20

America's Industrial Revolution Quiz 21

Revolution in Transportation and
    Communication Quiz 22

The Gilded Age Quiz 23

Effects of the Industrial Revolution Quiz 24

Teacher Lesson Plans for Language Arts

Vocabulary 25

Literature 25

Diaries 26

Readers' Theater 26

Student Activity Pages for Language Arts

Industrial Revolution Terms 27

Reading About History 28

Ashes of Roses 29

Lyddie 30

Diaries 31

Diary Evaluation 32

Readers' Theater Notes 33

Readers' Theater: Triangle Terror 34

Readers' Theater: Child's Work 36

**Teacher Lesson Plans for Social Studies and
    Science**

Time Line 38

Science Inventions and Projects 38

**Student Activity Pages for Social Studies and
    Science**

Time Line of the Industrial Revolution 39

Revolutionary Inventions 40

Electromagnets 41

Culminating Activities 44

Annotated Bibliography 45

Glossary 46

Answer Key 47

Introduction

The *Spotlight on America* series is designed to introduce students to significant events in American history. Reading in the content area is enriched with a variety of activities in language arts, literature, written and oral expression, social studies, and science. The series is designed to make history literally come alive in your classroom and take root in the minds of your students.

The Industrial Revolution was a transforming event in human history. It began in the mid-1700s in England and spread across Europe and America in the 1800s. With the advent of the Industrial Revolution, transportation changed from the plodding feet of horse-drawn coaches to swifter travel by steam-driven trains and ships. Communication was revolutionized as well with the invention of the telegraph and the telephone which replaced the slow, haphazard mail system of earlier times. Innovations in the manufacture of textiles, steel, food production, and a million other products changed life forever. The pace of change was accelerated even more by the introduction of electric power.

Although the Industrial Revolution led to inexpensive consumer goods and the mass production of virtually all goods, it was also accompanied by social and economic problems such as overcrowded tenements, child labor, and hazardous working conditions. Workers met tremendous opposition as they organized unions to protect themselves against powerful, greedy industrialists and giant corporations.

The reading selections in this book introduce the Industrial Revolution and also set the stage for activities in other subject areas. The literature readings expose students to the lives of people who suffered through and survived the turmoil created during the Industrial Revolution. The language arts and literature activities help students understand and sympathize with the problems that ordinary people faced during the first century of industrialization. The social studies and science activities help students recognize the importance of inventions as a major component of industrialization, and the culminating activities acquaint students with the way people lived during the age of industrial expansion.

Enjoy using this book with your students. Look for other books in this series.

ANDREW CARNEGIE   CORNELIUS VANDERBILT

J.P. MORGAN   JOHN D. ROCKEFELLER

Teacher Lesson Plans for Reading Comprehension

The Industrial Revolution Begins

Objective: Students will demonstrate fluency and comprehension in reading historically based text.

Materials: copies of The Industrial Revolution Begins (pages 7 and 8); copies of The Industrial Revolution Begins Quiz (page 20); additional reading selections from books, encyclopedias, and Internet sources for enrichment

Procedure

1. Reproduce and distribute The Industrial Revolution Begins. Review pre-reading skills by briefly reviewing the text and encouraging students to underline, make notes in the margins, write questions, and highlight unfamiliar words as they read.

2. Have students read the article independently, in small groups, or together as a class.

3. As a class, discuss the following questions or others of your choosing.

   • How did the Industrial Revolution help consumers?

   • Why do you think the Industrial Revolution started with the manufacture of clothes rather than other products?

   • Which invention do you think was most important in bringing about the Industrial Revolution? Give your reasons.

Assessment: Have students complete The Industrial Revolution Begins Quiz. Correct the quiz together.

America's Industrial Revolution

Objective: Students will demonstrate fluency and comprehension in reading historically based text.

Materials: copies of America's Industrial Revolution (pages 9 and 10); copies of America's Industrial Revolution Quiz (page 21); additional reading selections from books, encyclopedias, and Internet sources for enrichment

Procedure

1. Reproduce and distribute America's Industrial Revolution. Review pre-reading skills by briefly reviewing the text and encouraging students to underline, make notes in the margins, write questions, and highlight unfamiliar words as they read.

2. Have students read the article independently, in small groups, or together as a class.

3. As a class, discuss the following questions or others of your choosing.

   • Which vision of America do you think is better—Thomas Jefferson's nation of farmers or Alexander Hamilton's nation of factories? Why?

   • Did the textile mills of the early 1800s help girls or take advantage of them?

   • Why are inventions important to a nation?

Assessment: Have students complete America's Industrial Revolution Quiz. Correct the quiz together.

Teacher Lesson Plans for Reading Comprehension *(cont.)*

Revolution in Transportation and Communication

Objective: Students will demonstrate fluency and comprehension in reading historically based text.

Materials: copies of Revolution in Transportation and Communication (pages 11–13); copies of Revolution in Transportation and Communication Quiz (page 22); additional reading selections from books, encyclopedias, and Internet sources for enrichment

Procedure

1. Reproduce and distribute Revolution in Transportation and Communication. Review pre-reading skills by briefly reviewing the text and encouraging students to underline, make notes in the margins, write questions, and highlight unfamiliar words as they read.
2. Have students read the article independently, in small groups, or together as a class.
3. As a class, discuss the following questions or others of your choosing.
   - What was the most important advancement in transportation? Give your reasons.
   - Which was more important—the telegraph or telephone? Explain.
   - What were some of the difficulties involved in travel in the 1800s which you would not have liked?

Assessment: Have students complete the Revolution in Transportation and Communication Quiz. Correct the quiz together.

The Gilded Age

Objective: Students will demonstrate fluency and comprehension in reading historically based text.

Materials: copies of The Gilded Age (pages 14–16); copies of The Gilded Age Quiz (page 23); additional reading selections from books, encyclopedias, and Internet sources for enrichment

Procedure

1. Reproduce and distribute The Gilded Age. Review pre-reading skills by briefly reviewing the text and encouraging students to underline, make notes in the margins, write questions, and highlight unfamiliar words as they read.
2. Have students read the article independently, in small groups, or together as a class.
3. As a class, discuss the following questions or others of your choosing.
   - Do you think any businesses today operate as the trusts did during the Gilded Age? Explain your answer.
   - Which baron of the Gilded Age is most interesting to you? Why?
   - What could workers have done to improve their working conditions? Did they have any real options?

Assessment: Have students complete The Gilded Age Quiz. Correct the quiz together.

Teacher Lesson Plans for Reading Comprehension *(cont.)*

Effects of the Industrial Revolution

Objective: Students will demonstrate fluency and comprehension in reading historically based text.

Materials: copies of Effects of the Industrial Revolution (pages 17–19); copies of Effects of the Industrial Revolution Quiz (page 24); additional reading selections from books, encyclopedias, and Internet sources for enrichment

Procedure

1. Reproduce and distribute the Effects of the Industrial Revolution. Review pre-reading skills by briefly reviewing the text and encouraging students to underline, make notes in the margins, write questions, and highlight unfamiliar words as they read.

2. Have students read the article independently, in small groups, or together as a class.

3. As a class, discuss the following questions or others of your choosing.

    • How would you feel if you had been a child laborer in a factory or mine in the early 1900s?

    • What could workers do to protect themselves against the power of giant trusts?

    • Why are tenements and other slum housing dangerous to those who live there?

Assessment: Have students complete the Effects of the Industrial Revolution Quiz. Correct the quiz together.

Reading
Passages

The Industrial Revolution Begins

Beginnings in Britain

The Industrial Revolution is one of the most important events in human history. It changed people's lives in every part of the world, affected the fortunes of nations, and dramatically altered the planet itself. This revolution began in England in the mid-1700s because of the unique set of circumstances which existed in that country. It was spurred by several inventions which made it possible to produce cloth cheaply. The revolution was fed by the power of Great Britain which was one of the dominant powers in the world and had huge markets in its colonies. In addition, Britain had ample supplies of coal and iron but little useable farm land.

Homegrown and Homemade

Before the Industrial Revolution, most families in Great Britain lived on farms, which were usually owned by large landowners. People made their own clothes and grew their own food. Women spun thread on a simple spinning wheel and then made homespun clothes from wool gotten by shearing their own sheep. It was a long and exhausting process.

Most people had few clothes other than what they were actually wearing. Washing clothes was rarely done because the cloth deteriorated badly—both from being washed and from being allowed to get so sweaty, oily, and filthy in daily wear. People grew what they ate or traded food for other necessities. Money was scarce, and there were few opportunities to earn it.

Cottage Industry

The Industrial Revolution began as a revolutionary way of making clothes. Businessmen in England in the mid-1700s began to buy wool and other materials and source it out to women who worked in their homes to spin the thread, make cloth, and then sew clothes. Because the work was done at home, it became known as a *cottage industry*. Family members helped. This provided extra money for the family, and businessmen did not need to have a factory. This system gradually changed as better machines for making cloth were developed, which created the textile industry and brought about the Industrial Revolution.

Spinning Weel

 Reading Passages # The Industrial Revolution Begins *(cont.)*

Better Spinning Machines

The spinning wheel had existed for centuries. It was a simple, foot-powered instrument which produced one thread at a time. Many efforts were made to improve this tool, but most were unsuccessful. The invention of the flying shuttle in 1733 by a mechanic named John Kay allowed weavers to create much more cloth than they had been able to before. Then in the late 1760s, James Hargreaves invented the spinning jenny which could spin eight threads at a time instead of just one.

Richard Arkwright then invented a spinning frame which made even more threads but was too large to keep in a home. He built a factory to house the horse-powered machine and hired people to work in the factory. In 1785 Edmund Cartwright invented a water-powered loom which greatly increased the speed of weaving. It too required a factory.

Steam-Powered Engines

The most significant invention of this period was the steam engine invented by Thomas Newcomen in 1712 and substantially improved by James Watt in the late 1770s. This engine did not require running water or horses to provide energy. Steam engines could be built and installed in factories almost anywhere. The development of steam engines led to major improvements in making machinery tools, which in turn led to these tools being used to create new and better versions of engines and many other machines.

Coal and Iron

The two great resources of the Industrial Age were coal and iron. Coal was essential in providing the power to make a steam engine work. Massive amounts of coal were used to power these engines, and England had many available coal mines. Coal also became vital to the production of iron. Heating coal in an air-tight oven produces coke, and in 1713 an English iron maker used coke to make iron (instead of using hardwood from England's nearly depleted forests). Further inventions made it easier to make iron as well as to make it stronger, simpler to work with, and easier to roll into the needed shapes.

On to America

After beginning in England, the Industrial Revolution spread to France, Belgium, Germany, and other European countries. The United States—having newly gained its independence from England—became fertile ground for the spread of industrialization. Many of the northern states in the U.S. began to experience a spurt in the development of factories. From 1783 until 1860, factories spread throughout the country. The Civil War and years that followed brought the United States to a position of world power, based on its industrial might.

 Reading Passages

America's Industrial Revolution

Stolen Knowledge

It was illegal to reveal or distribute information about England's textile machinery, methods, or setup to other nations and even to England's own colonies. The colonies were expected to supply raw materials, but the manufacturing was to be done in England. The penalties for violating these state secrets were severe.

Samuel Slater was a 21-year-old former apprentice to a textile manufacturer who wanted to go to the newly independent United States to start his own textile business. He knew that there were businessmen in America who were interested in building textile factories. Because he could not chance being caught with written notes or diagrams, Slater memorized the internal machinery of spinning and weaving machines. He then disguised himself as a farmer and sailed to America in September 1789. He had no money, but he carried a fortune in his memory. Slater soon found a partner, Moses Brown, who had the necessary money, and together they opened the first American textile mill in Rhode Island.

Two American Viewpoints

The new American nation had two competing self-images. One view, which was expressed by Thomas Jefferson, perceived the United States as an agricultural nation populated primarily by farmers who owned and farmed small parcels of land. This ideal would persist in American minds into the late 20th century, long after the nation had few farm families left on the land. Jefferson did not want the United States to become a nation of factories because he had personally witnessed the suffering of factory workers in England.

The second image was envisioned by Alexander Hamilton, a friend of U.S. President George Washington and the new secretary of the treasury. Hamilton wanted the country to industrialize rapidly. He wanted the United States to build factories because it would encourage immigration to the country, increase the value of farm products since there would be more people to buy the products, and greatly strengthen the nation as a world power able to compete with other nations. Eventually, Hamilton's policies would succeed.

Alexander Hamilton

 Reading Passages

America's Industrial Revolution *(cont.)*

Invention Leads the Way

Inventors are more likely to spend time creating and testing new ideas if they are going to make money from their efforts. The new government of the United States passed a patent law in 1790 which ensured inventors' legal control over their inventions and the sale of these inventions for 17 years. The first 10 years saw fewer than 300 patents (rights to an invention) issued to inventors. However, after 1800 the number rose dramatically.

Unfortunately the patent law did not always protect an inventor. In 1793 Eli Whitney invented the cotton gin, which separated the seeds from cotton 50 times faster than could be done by hand. Since the machine was easy to duplicate, many planters simply made their own cotton gins. As a result, Whitney and his partner were unable to protect his invention.

The cotton gin led to a far greater supply of cotton for the new textile factories in the North. It also helped keep slavery as an institution in the South because slaves were needed to grow and harvest the cotton.

Cotton Gin

Working Girls

Textile factory owners in Massachusetts found that they could hire farm girls to work in their factories for about $3 a week, depending upon their experience and effort. Although the wages were low, it was more than the girls could make as seamstresses or servants, who made less than a dollar a week. As a result, thousands of single girls worked in the mills for a few years until they married. They lived in company-owned boarding houses where they paid about a third of their earnings for rent and food. The girls followed strict rules both at the factories and at the boarding houses, but many young women preferred this life to the drudgery of the farm.

Men who worked in the factories were paid twice as much as the girls but were often hard for manufacturers to keep. Most young American men preferred to take a chance on farming with the hope of owning land and becoming independent. Businessmen encouraged immigration because many of the people arriving from other countries were grateful for the chance to get any kind of job. Life was better for American factory workers than it was for the struggling and often unemployed people in Europe.

 Reading Passages

Revolution in Transportation and Communication

National Roads

Factories produce goods, but the ability to transport these goods to buyers is essential to the growth of industry. In the early 1800s the only cheap and efficient means of travel was by water. It was far cheaper to send a ton of cotton from North Carolina to England than it was to ship it a few hundred miles to Pennsylvania. The U.S. government addressed this problem by funding a National Road from Cumberland, Maryland, through what is now Wheeling, West Virginia, and eventually all the way to Vandalia, Illinois. This wagon road helped owners transport goods west to buyers who would otherwise not have been able to purchase them.

Canals

The Erie Canal was dug across central New York State and helped manufacturers reach western buyers. Built between 1817 and 1825, the Erie Canal was a major engineering accomplishment of the era. Shipping goods on this man-made waterway cut the cost of shipping to a fraction of what it cost to transport freight by wagon along rugged trails and roads. Over 13,000 boats used the canal in its first year of operation. The success of the Erie Canal encouraged many other states to dig canals connecting natural waterways.

Steamboats

Flatboats were modified rafts which were very effective for moving products downriver. They allowed farmers to ship goods down the Ohio and Mississippi rivers to New Orleans, but there was no effective way to ship goods upstream until the invention of the steamboat. Early inventors of steamboats, such as John Fitch, actually lost money because so few people were willing to take a chance riding on such unusual looking boats and because they feared the engines would explode. The first steamboats were not big enough or strong enough to carry large loads.

Robert Fulton

Robert Fulton improved the design of the steamboat. In addition, he used copper sheets to build the huge boiler which was needed to power such a large boat. Fulton demonstrated his invention by carrying a load up the Hudson River from New York City to Albany at five miles an hour, much faster than any flatboat or wagon could travel. He named his ship the *Clermont*. The success of Fulton's steamboat led to the rapid production of many of these boats.

Reading
Passages

Revolution in Transportation and Communication (cont.)

Speedy Steamboats

Steamboats became synonymous with speedy water travel although they were very slow by today's standards. A trip from New Orleans, Louisiana, to Louisville, Kentucky, took three months by land but only about 10 days by steamboat. Investors were impressed with this invention, and many steamboats were made.

Travel on these boats remained popular even with frequent accidents, explosions, and drownings that killed hundreds of people during the age of steam. Steamboats were used on the ocean to travel from New York to London and especially on the waterways connecting the river cities of the American Midwest.

Railroads

Railroads changed forever the transportation of factory goods to local markets. The first railroads were cars pulled by horses along iron rails. The first steam locomotive was built by an English engineer named Richard Trevithick in 1804. A few other steam locomotives were built in England, but steam locomotives did not come into general use in England or America until the 1830s.

Some local rail lines had been built in New England with financing from local investors, but railroad lines needed more capital, or money, than private investors could raise.

In 1825 John Stevens built the first American-made railway steam engine. In 1831 an engine called the *DeWitt Clinton* traveled along New York rails at 15 miles per hour pulling cars that looked like converted horse carriages filled with factory goods. The locomotive was named after the New York governor who was chiefly responsible for the creation of the Erie Canal.

Businessmen convinced the U.S. Congress to provide funding, and by the 1850s railroad companies had been loaned millions of dollars and given over 130 million acres of land to use. These railroads made the transportation of factory products faster and much cheaper than any other form of land transportation. They also made possible the building of factories in more remote towns and cities.

Reading Passages

Revolution in Transportation and Communication *(cont.)*

Transcontinental Railroads

By 1860 the United States had more than 30,000 miles of railroad, and it was decided to build a transcontinental railroad to link the cities of the east with the west. The first transcontinental railroad connecting the Union Pacific and Central Pacific lines was completed in 1869. In the years that followed, railroad builders used government loans and land grants to build several transcontinental lines. The Great Northern Railroad connected the Northern cities of the Midwest and the far West. Several rail lines connected Midwestern and Southern cities to the cities in the American Southwest and California.

The Telegraph

A revolution was also taking place in communication in the United States. Samuel Morse invented the concept of the telegraph in the 1830s and finally managed to secure government funding for a telegraph line between Washington, DC, and Baltimore, Maryland, so that he could demonstrate the device. On May 24, 1844, Morse sent the first message — "What hath God wrought!"— on the new line. The telegraph immediately became popular, and by 1861 the United States had over 76,000 miles of telegraph lines. Many of these lines ran parallel to railroads.

The telegraph brought about another revolution in American life. Letters often took weeks to reach their destinations, and answers required more time before action could be taken. The telegraph allowed immediate response. Businessmen were now able to communicate instantly with customers, suppliers, and shippers throughout the nation. The telegraph also changed lives of average citizens who needed to communicate with relatives far away, and it radically altered the speed of military communication and operations.

Telegraph Machine

The Telephone

In 1876 Alexander Graham Bell invented the telephone. He formed the Bell Telephone Company the next year and in 1884 opened the first long-distance telephone service. Despite the expense, many merchants and factory owners were glad to pay for the opportunity to talk directly with suppliers and buyers. Thomas Edison improved the phone and made it able to handle more calls and be heard more clearly. By 1890 more than 19,000 operators were employed to handle calls.

 Reading Passages

The Gilded Age

U.S. Industrialization

In the United States, the Industrial Revolution reached a high point in the years from 1860 to 1900. The American Civil War provided a massive jump-start to the industrialization in the Northern states as they produced all of the essentials of war—from clothing to weapons. The period after the war became known as the *Gilded Age* because the rapid industrialization of the nation led to immense fortunes for a few businessmen who displayed their wealth through excessively lavish lifestyles.

Monopolies and Trusts

Every major industry seemed headed eventually toward *monopoly*, control by one company or person. Business leaders formed larger and larger monopolies called *trusts* which were able to control prices and wages by reducing competition. John D. Rockefeller controlled the petroleum (oil) business in the United States. Andrew Carnegie and Henry Clay Frick were giants in the steel business. J.P. Morgan was the major banker in the country and was so powerful that at times the U.S. government borrowed money from him. Cornelius Vanderbilt made his fortune in shipping and railroads.

Survival of the Fittest

The successful businessmen of the era had little concern for the workers who labored in their factories at the lowest possible wages. They used ruthless policies to crush other businesses and even cut prices below cost if it served to destroy a smaller competitor.

Industry giants made illegal deals with suppliers of raw materials to cut off the competition, and they arranged favorable rebates for themselves with railroads and shippers who wanted their business. The trusts threatened to quit dealing with businesses that also dealt with their competitors, and they prevented competitors from getting favorable bank loans. They even corrupted government officials with bribes. In fact, Americans began to wonder who some politicians worked for—the industrialists or the American people.

Exploiting the Land

The big trusts took advantage in other ways too. Since there was little concern for the environment, they had access to cheap natural resources. They also managed to gain control of land, whether it belonged to private individuals or the government. The trusts often used their powerful legal teams to defeat individual landowners in court. In less-settled areas, powerful trusts just took possession of land and shoved the farmers or prospectors out of the way. In the case of railroads, millions of acres of free land were given to them by the government as payment for laying the tracks.

The Gilded Age (cont.)

Labor Beaten

Because they needed work when they came to the U.S., many immigrants were forced to work long hours for wages that were barely enough to survive on. When workers tried to organize *strikes* (work stoppages) to protest, the giant trusts hired thugs and law enforcement officers to break up the strikes and beat up the striking workers. The business owners often controlled the courts which, in turn, supported their ruthless behavior. Factory workers were powerless. If they did not work, many unemployed workers were willing to take their jobs.

Robber Barons

Robber baron is a term used to describe industrialists in the late 19th century who dominated their industries and accumulated huge personal fortunes, generally through unfair business practices. These barons claimed they made the United States more productive and economically stronger, but it was done at the expense of their workers. While they lived in huge mansions, their employees lived in extreme poverty.

John D. Rockefeller

Born in 1839, John D. Rockefeller went to work at the age of 16 as an assistant bookkeeper. Hard-working and thrifty, he used his savings to establish an oil refinery in the mid-1860s and quickly became a major power in the newly developing oil industry. He started the Standard Oil Company in 1870. The company soon began to merge with other companies and to destroy competitors who had higher costs than Standard Oil. By the 1880s, Rockefeller controlled most of the petroleum industry. He was also heavily involved in finance, railroads, and other industries.

Rockefeller retired with an immense fortune in 1911 and donated money to many causes. He founded the University of Chicago, the Rockefeller Institute for Medical Research, and the Rockefeller Foundation which promoted public health and medical research. His monopolistic oil corporation, Standard Oil, was broken up by court order in 1911, and 37 new companies were formed from it.

Andrew Carnegie

Andrew Carnegie was an immigrant from Scotland who came to the United States in 1848 when he was 12 years old. His father was a weaver, and his mother stitched shoe leather. At the age of 12, Andrew worked as a bobbin boy in a cotton factory. Later he became a telegraph messenger, railroad clerk, secretary to the assistant secretary of war, and superintendent of a railroad.

Carnegie invested in several businesses which became profitable, and he became convinced that steel would replace iron in heavy manufacturing. By 1892 the Carnegie Steel Company was the largest steel company in the world. Carnegie's company continued to grow until he sold out to U.S. Steel. His fortune was estimated at a quarter of a billion dollars. Carnegie financed more than 3,000 public libraries, an international peace organization, and science foundations.

Reading Passages

The Gilded Age *(cont.)*

Henry Clay Frick

Henry Clay Frick was a farmer, storekeeper, and an accountant before he and several associates organized a company to operate coke ovens. (*Coke* is treated coal used to make steel.) Frick bought out several struggling competitors during a depression in 1873 and became a major figure in the industry. Steel-maker Andrew Carnegie bought a substantial portion of Frick's coke business, and Frick acquired stock in Carnegie's steel business.

Frick became chairman of the steel company and later organized the Carnegie Steel Company. He was ruthless in suppressing unions. The conflict between the steel company and the unions came to a head in the bitter Homestead strike in 1892 when union men and strike breakers fought for control. Frick smashed the union and set an anti-labor policy in the steel industry that lasted for decades. Frick clashed with Carnegie over policy in 1899 but was later a director of U.S. Steel, formed from the Carnegie company.

J.P. Morgan

John Pierpont Morgan was born in 1837. He became the most powerful figure in finance and industry during the industrial age. He was a genius in using investment money to create industrial monopolies which made huge profits. Morgan bought out Andrew Carnegie and set up the first billion-dollar corporation, U.S. Steel.

Morgan controlled the economy of the nation with the assets invested in his financial empire. He used his influence to prevent at least three major financial panics, which saved many American investors from losing everything they owned. He even loaned money to the U.S. government when necessary. At his death, Morgan was worth 80 million dollars—less than a tenth of Rockefeller's fortune.

Cornelius Vanderbilt

Born in 1794, Cornelius Vanderbilt built his fortune on steamship and railroad empires. He began with a ferry service in New York and expanded it into an international steamship business. During the California Gold Rush of 1849, Vanderbilt opened a shipping line from the East coast to California that used an overland route across Nicaragua which saved 600 miles, cut the price in half, and earned him over $1 million a year.

When he was almost 70, Vanderbilt decided that railroads were the wave of the future. He acquired the Central Railroad in 1867 and extended the line to Chicago. By 1875 his New York Central Railroad controlled the profitable route between New York and Chicago, reportedly clearing $25 million in the first five years. He established Vanderbilt University but was snubbed by New York City high society, who said he was a rich but vulgar man. At his death, Vanderbilt had a fortune of $95 million.

Effects of the Industrial Revolution

Economic and Social Changes

The Industrial Revolution created massive economic and social changes in every nation. In the United States and other countries, the middle class made rapid economic progress. Some invested in the new businesses or became managers. As customers, they benefited from the cheaper prices for clothing and other factory products.

The need for engineers, accountants, managers, and other professionals led to an increase in education for middle-class students able to afford college. Many American colleges were built in the new western states and financed by land grants. Colleges became the training grounds for a new class of professionals and business leaders.

Tenements

The growth of industry led to crowded cities as immigrants and others settled there to get work. Cities soon became filled with *tenements*. These apartments for working families were overcrowded, poorly built, filthy, and dangerous.

Disease spread rapidly through these slum areas. Water had to be carried in buckets up the stairs to the apartments. Children slept two or three to a bed, and there was no privacy. Kerosene and coal were used for heating. Fires were commonplace and often destroyed entire blocks of apartments. Crime was a constant problem.

Crowded Cities and Empty Farms

Even though the American frontier was being populated by farmers, larger cities were growing even faster. By the end of the 19th century, the American frontier was settled, but most Americans lived in cities. In the first 50 years of the 20th century, Americans left the farms and moved to the cities for better job opportunities. By 1980 only a very small percentage of Americans lived on farms.

The Working Class

Factory workers labored 12 to 14 hours a day, six days a week. They got Sundays off for religious reasons, but holidays and vacations were unheard of. There was no sick leave, and workers often lost their jobs if they did not show up to work—regardless of the reason. Contagious diseases spread in the cramped and unsanitary conditions of the factories. Accidents were common, and crippled workers simply lost their jobs.

Business owners kept wages as low as possible and docked a worker's pay for the smallest infraction such as being a few minutes late, accidentally breaking a machine, or not working fast enough. Some owners even believed that higher wages would make workers lazy and unproductive.

Effects of the Industrial Revolution *(cont.)*

Child Labor

Since there were no laws against children working in factories, boys and girls under 10 years old were routinely employed in textile mills—often in very dangerous jobs. Because they were small and agile, some children were used to run under machines and tie loose threads. Boys as young as seven years old worked as *doffers*, replacing the bobbins of thread in textile factories. Girls of the same age worked as *spinners*, brushing lint from machines and tying broken threads. Many children developed spinal deformities, limps, and other physical injuries from their work.

In coal mines, boys as young as 10 years old were allowed to work separating the slate and stone from the coal on moving troughs. Many fell into the river of coal and were mangled or killed. All had coughs from breathing the coal dust. At the age of 12, they graduated to work in the mines.

Immigrant children worked along with their parents in canneries shucking oysters, cutting beans, peeling apples and tomatoes, and processing other foods. Most child workers had no schooling. They worked 12 to 14 hours a day just like adults.

School was not mandatory, and many families desperately needed the money their children earned in order to eat. Children earned less than half of what adult men were paid.

Women in the Factories

Many American farm girls, especially in New England in the early 1800s, worked in factories for a few years before they married. These working girls earned about $3 a week and had to pay part of that for room and board. Later women and girls from immigrant families, as well as some American-born women, worked in textile factories to help support their families. They worked as long and as hard as the men but were paid about half their wages.

Unemployment

Severe depressions and business collapses in the 1870s and 1890s cost many people their jobs. Many families lived week-to-week, and a lost day for a worker meant less food on the table. Weeks and months of unemployment meant starvation and homelessness. Families lost their apartments when they could not pay the rent. Some families received charity from churches, but most simply suffered and tried to find whatever odd jobs they could, usually at even lower pay.

Reading Passages

Effects of the Industrial Revolution *(cont.)*

The Growth of Unions

The steel industrialist Andrew Carnegie said, "The worker has no more to do with setting his wages than does a piece of coal with setting its price." The attitude of business owners that workers could do nothing about their situation was usually accurate. Factory workers tried to organize unions throughout the 19th century and especially in the 1890s, but they faced a severe uphill battle.

Many workers were afraid of losing their jobs and therefore did not support unions. When the unions tried to strike, *scabs* (unemployed workers) were brought in by the owners to take the jobs. Strikers were often beaten by hired thugs and professional strike breakers. Police and federal troops were sometimes used in large strikes to support the business owners.

No Political Support

Factory workers had little political influence for several reasons. Many legislators were bribed or had business interests of their own which made them sympathetic to the powerful trusts. Women, children, and immigrants could not vote. The workers who could vote did not have enough votes to make a difference.

A Second Industrial Revolution

The first half of the 20th century witnessed a second industrial revolution with massive growth in manufacturing due to new inventions, better transportation, and the impact of World War I and World War II. This second period of industrialization was also characterized by the rise of labor unions which had political influence.

The trusts were brought under control in part by President Theodore Roosevelt, whose tough policies limited their influence. He was concerned that these trusts exercised more authority than the U.S. government. Later presidents like Franklin Delano Roosevelt and Harry Truman also tried to limit the power of monopolies. The Great Depression in the 1930s made American voters distrustful of the powerful trusts and also led to legislation curtailing their influence.

A New Industrial Age

Today industrialization is on the rise in countries like China and India. In an attempt to reduce labor costs, many American and European companies are sending work to countries where laborers work for lower wages and fewer benefits. These workers often labor in poor conditions similar to those during America's early industrial age. The process of industrialization may continue for decades as other countries encounter their own industrial revolution.

The Industrial Revolution Begins Quiz

Directions: Read pages 7 and 8 about the beginning of the Industrial Revolution. Answer each question below by circling the correct answer.

1. In what country did the Industrial Revolution begin?
   a. England
   b. France
   c. United States
   d. Germany

2. What was the first product to be produced by the new machines and methods of the Industrial Revolution?
   a. food
   b. steel
   c. clothes
   d. cars

3. Which resources did Great Britain have that helped encourage the development of industry?
   a. land and water
   b. people and farms
   c. sheep and cattle
   d. coal and iron

4. What does the word *textile* mean?
   a. food
   b. cloth
   c. iron
   d. oil

5. What material is heated in an air-tight oven to make coke?
   a. iron
   b. steel
   c. coal
   d. clothing

6. What increased the production of cloth in the 1700s?
   a. spinning jenny
   b. flying shuttle
   c. water-powered loom
   d. all of the above

7. What was the most significant invention of the Industrial Revolution?
   a. steam engine
   b. coal
   c. spinning frame
   d. automobiles

8. Which inventor improved the steam engine?
   a. James Kay
   b. Richard Arkwright
   c. Edmund Cartwright
   d. James Watt

9. Which raw material was essential to the production of iron?
   a. wool
   b. coal
   c. oil
   d. cotton

10. Which conditions were important in the development of the Industrial Revolution?
    a. new inventions
    b. plentiful supplies of coal
    c. plentiful supply of iron
    d. all of the above

America's Industrial Revolution Quiz

Directions: Read pages 9 and 10 about the beginning of the Industrial Revolution in America. Answer each question below by circling the correct answer.

1. Why did Samuel Slater memorize the details of textile machines to come to the United States?
   a. He could not write.
   b. It was illegal to have diagrams.
   c. They were state secrets.
   d. both b and c

2. Where was the first textile mill in the U.S. built?
   a. New York
   b. New Jersey
   c. Massachusetts
   d. Rhode Island

3. What invention made it more profitable to grow cotton?
   a. steel plow
   b. cotton gin
   c. spinning wheel
   d. factories

4. Who invented the cotton gin?
   a. Eli Whitney
   b. Moses Brown
   c. Samuel Slater
   d. Alexander Hamilton

5. What was the weekly salary of mill girls in Massachusetts?
   a. $3
   b. $30
   c. $1
   d. $300

6. How much money did the mill girls pay for rent and food?
   a. $3
   b. $1
   c. $2
   d. $100

7. What workers made less than a dollar a week?
   a. mill girls
   b. seamstresses
   c. servants
   d. both b and c

8. Which leader wanted the U.S. to become an industrial nation?
   a. Thomas Jefferson
   b. George Washington
   c. Alexander Hamilton
   d. Eli Whitney

9. Who believed that the U.S. should remain a nation of small farms?
   a. Alexander Hamilton
   b. George Washington
   c. Thomas Jefferson
   d. Moses Brown

10. What guarantees an inventor legal protection for his invention?
   a. gin
   b. contract
   c. trade
   d. patent

Revolution in Transportation and Communication Quiz

Directions: Read pages 11–13 about the development of transportation and communication in America. Answer each question below by circling the correct answer.

1. Who designed a steamboat for carrying many goods and people?
   a. Samuel Morse
   b. DeWitt Clinton
   c. Robert Fulton
   d. John Fitch

2. What invention sent the message "What hath God wrought!"?
   a. railroad
   b. telephone
   c. steamboat
   d. telegraph

3. What was built to connect U.S. cities in the East and West?
   a. canals
   b. steamboats
   c. transcontinental railroad
   d. flatboats

4. What was the fastest means of travel from New Orleans, Louisiana, to Louisville, Kentucky?
   a. telegraph
   b. flatboat
   c. horseback
   d. steamboat

5. Why was the Erie Canal important?
   a. It was a natural passageway.
   b. It was faster than land routes.
   c. It was an engineering success.
   d. all of the above

6. Which invention in the 1830s speeded up communication?
   a. telegraph
   b. telephone
   c. railroad
   d. steamboat

7. Who invented the telephone?
   a. Alexander Graham Bell
   b. John Stevens
   c. DeWitt Clinton
   d. Robert Fulton

8. How was the building of railroads financed?
   a. government funding
   b. private investment
   c. land grants to railroads
   d. all of the above

9. In which Midwestern state did the National Road end?
   a. Maryland
   b. West Virginia
   c. Illinois
   d. California

10. To whom was the telegraph important?
    a. military
    b. businesses
    c. average citizens
    d. all of the above

The Gilded Age Quiz

Directions: Read pages 14–16 about the years called the Gilded Age in America. Answer each question below by circling the correct answer.

1. Which event provided a massive jump-start to the industrialization of the United States?
   a. World War I
   b. Civil War
   c. the discovery of oil
   d. the frontier

2. Which businessman created the Standard Oil Company?
   a. John D. Rockefeller
   b. Andrew Carnegie
   c. Henry Clay Frick
   d. J.P. Morgan

3. What name was given to the period after the Civil War when rapid industrialization led to huge fortunes for some?
   a. Gilded Age
   b. Age of Labor
   c. American Frontier
   d. Industrial Age

4. Which immigrant from Scotland became the owner of the largest steel company in America?
   a. J.P. Morgan
   b. Andrew Carnegie
   c. Henry Clay Frick
   d. John D. Rockefeller

5. Who made his fortune in steamships and railroads?
   a. John D. Rockefeller
   b. Henry Clay Frick
   c. Cornelius Vanderbilt
   d. J.P. Morgan

6. What happens in a monopoly?
   a. One person or company is in control.
   b. Prices and wages are fixed.
   c. Competitiors are forced out.
   d. all of the above

7. Which businessman financed more than 3,000 public libraries?
   a. J.P. Morgan
   b. Andrew Carnegie
   c. E.H. Harriman
   d. John D. Rockefeller

8. Who was so powerful that he even loaned money to the U.S. government?
   a. John D. Rockefeller
   b. Henry Clay Frick
   c. Andrew Carnegie
   d. J.P. Morgan

9. What term describes industrialists who got rich through unfair business practices?
   a. robber barons
   b. scabs
   c. strike breakers
   d. investors

10. Which monopoly was broken up into 37 new companies in 1911?
    a. Standard Oil
    b. U.S. Steel
    c. Carnegie Steel
    d. Union Pacific

Effects of the Industrial Revolution Quiz

Directions: Read pages 17–19 about the effects of the Industrial Revolution. Answer each question below by circling the correct answer.

1. Which group of people benefited the most from the Industrial Revolution?
   a. mill workers
   b. farmers
   c. the middle class
   d. immigrants

2. Which word refers to overcrowded apartments for working families?
   a. immigrants
   b. tenements
   c. unsanitary
   d. chutes

3. How many hours a day did people work in a factory?
   a. 12 to 14
   b. 4 to 6
   c. 6 to 10
   d. 8

4. Who replaced bobbins of thread in a textile factory?
   a. miners
   b. scabs
   c. cripples
   d. children

5. What term was used to describe unemployed workers hired to take the jobs of union people on strike?
   a. scabs
   b. spinners
   c. doffers
   d. trusts

6. In what country is the process of industrialization still developing?
   a. United States
   b. India
   c. China
   d. both b and c

7. What created a second industrial revolution in the United States in the first half of the 20th century?
   a. new inventions
   b. the impact of two world wars
   c. better transportation
   d. all of the above

8. Why did factory workers have little political support at first?
   a. Immigrants could not vote.
   b. They did not care about politics.
   c. Women could not vote.
   d. both a and c

9. School attendance was not mandatory in some states. What does *mandatory* mean?
   a. allowed
   b. required
   c. invented
   d. tardy

10. What are contagious diseases?
    a. surgeries
    b. easily spread to others
    c. drug abuse
    d. incurable

Teacher Lesson Plans for Language Arts

Vocabulary

Objective: Students will learn to apply language arts skills in vocabulary enrichment.

Materials: copies of Industrial Revolution Terms (page 27)

Procedure

1. Reproduce and distribute Industrial Revolution Terms. Review the vocabulary and pronunciation if necessary. Have students do the assigned page.

2. An optional activity would be to have students write sentences using each of the 20 vocabulary words listed on this page. As an alternative, students could write a paragraph or short story using the vocabulary words.

Assessment: Correct the activity sheet with the students. Evaluate students' correct usage of vocabulary words if the optional activity is assigned.

Literature

Objective: Students will read and respond to works of historical nonfiction and historical novels that are based upon the experiences of people who lived during the Industrial Revolution.

Materials: copies of Reading About History (page 28); copies of *Ashes of Roses* (page 29); copies of *Lyddie* (page 30); copies of the books *Immigrant Kids, Kids at Work: Lewis Hine and the Crusade Against Child Labor*, and *Good Girl Work: Factories, Sweatshops, and How Women Changed Their Role in the American Workplace* (see page 28); copies of the books *Ashes of Roses* (see page 29) and *Lyddie* (see page 30) as well as other nonfiction books or novels listed in the bibliography on page 45

Procedure

1. Reproduce and distribute Reading About History (page 28). Help students choose an appropriate book. Instruct them to read the book and then complete the nonfiction report form, Women and Children in the Industrial Revolution, at the bottom of the page. Allow time for students to share what they learned with the class.

2. Reproduce and distribute *Ashes of Roses* (page 29). Have students read the book as a class or on their own. Then have them write answers to the comprehension questions on a separate sheet of paper. As a class or in small groups, let them share responses to the discussion questions.

3. Reproduce and distribute *Lyddie* (page 30). Have students read the book independently or as a class. When finished, have them answer the Comprehension Questions on a separate sheet of paper. As a class or in small groups, have them share responses to the Discussion Questions.

Assessment: Use the nonfiction report form, answers to comprehension questions, and class discussions to assess student performance on the literature selections.

Teacher Lesson Plans for Language Arts *(cont.)*

Diaries

Objective: Students will learn to apply language arts skills in reading and understanding the diary format.

Materials: copies of Diaries (page 31) and Diary Evaluation (page 32)

Procedure

1. Reproduce and distribute copies of both Diaries and Diary Evaluation. Have students select a diary to read from those listed on the page (or another one about the Industrial Revolution with teacher approval).

2. Instruct students to complete the diary evaluation.

3. As an extension, have students write a letter to a friend or relative in another country who is planning to come to the United States to work. Using what they have already learned, students should briefly describe the living and working conditions in America.

Assessment: Review students' diary evaluations and letters.

Readers' Theater

Objective: Students will learn to use their voices effectively in dramatic reading.

Materials: copies of Readers' Theater Notes (page 33); copies of Readers' Theater: Triangle Terror (pages 34 and 35); copies of Readers' Theater: Child's Work (pages 36 and 37)

Procedure

1. Reproduce and distribute the Readers' Theater Notes. Review the basic concept of a readers' theater with the class.

2. Reproduce and distribute Readers' Theater: Triangle Terror and Readers' Theater: Child's Work. Assign students to small groups, and give them several days to practice reading the script together.

3. Schedule class performances, and have students share the prepared scripts.

4. As an extension, have students use the suggestions on the bottom of page 33 to write their own readers' theater. Allow time for them to write and practice their scripts. Then have them present their plays to the class.

Assessment: Base performance assessments on performers' pacing, volume, expression, and focus. Student-created scripts should demonstrate general writing skills, dramatic tension, and a good plot.

| 1650 | 1700 | 1750 | 1800 | 1850 | 1900 |

Industrial Revolution Terms

Directions: Match each term in Column 1 with its correct meaning in Column 2. Use the glossary in the back of this book or a dictionary to help you.

Column 1

_____ 1. canal

_____ 2. coal

_____ 3. factory

_____ 4. immigrant

_____ 5. industrialization

_____ 6. manufacture

_____ 7. patent

_____ 8. raw materials

_____ 9. robber barons

_____ 10. slum

_____ 11. strike

_____ 12. textile

Column 2

a. work stoppage by workers

b. legal protection for an inventor

c. basic resources used to make things

d. cloth

e. ruthless businessmen

f. building where products are made

g. a person who moves to another country to live

h. to make a product

i. run-down housing lived in by the poor

j. use of machines to do tasks formerly done by human and animal power

k. a man-made waterway

l. a black mineral found in the earth

Directions: Use the terms below to complete these sentences.

| capital | loom | monopoly | tenement |
| competition | mill | steam engine | union |

13. A _____ is a machine used to weave thread into cloth.

14. Businesses needed _____ to buy machinery and hire workers.

15. The Standard Oil Corporation was a _____ because it controlled the oil industry.

16. A _____ is a factory where products like textiles or steel are manufactured.

17. Many factories got their power from a _____.

18. Members of a _____ sometimes strike in order to get higher pay and better working conditions.

19. When businesses are in _____, they try hard to offer lower prices and better service.

20. A _____ is run-down housing for poor people.

Reading About History

Some writers recreate the history of a period so well that it reads like an illustrated novel. Russell Freedman and Catherine Gourley are two such authors.

Assignment

Read one of the nonfiction books listed below or another one that tells about life and working conditions for women and children during the Industrial Revolution. Then complete the report form below.

Freedman, Russell. *Immigrant Kids.* Scholastic, 1980. (Superior account of the lives of immigrant children in America at work, in school, and at home)

Freedman, Russell. *Kids at Work: Lewis Hine and the Crusade Against Child Labor.* Clarion, 1994. (The story of the schoolteacher-photographer whose vivid black-and-white portraits of child laborers helped to finally end the practice of young children working in factories, coal mines, and cotton fields)

Gourley, Catherine. *Good Girl Work: Factories, Sweatshops, and How Women Changed Their Role in the American Workplace.* Millbrook, 1999. (An exceptionally clear account of the lives of factory girls during the Industrial Revolution)

Women and Children in the Industrial Revolution

List and describe at least five jobs done by women and children in factories or mines.

1. _____
2. _____
3. _____
4. _____
5. _____

Give three examples of how women and children were treated.

1. _____
2. _____
3. _____

What did you learn from reading this book? How do you feel about the treatment of women and children in the work force during this period?

_____

_____

_____

Ashes of Roses

The fire at the Triangle Shirtwaist Factory in March 1911 killed 146 women workers. It also made the rest of the nation vitally aware of how workers were being mistreated. The book *Ashes of Roses* by Mary Jane Auch tells about this horrible tragedy from the viewpoint of Rose, a teenage immigrant who worked in the factory.

Comprehension Questions

Read the book *Ashes of Roses*. Then answer the following questions on a separate sheet of paper.

1. From what country does Rose emigrate to live in the United States?
2. Why could Joseph not stay in the United States?
3. What was the buttonhook exam?
4. What are *greenhorns*?
5. What is Rose's first job?
6. Who is Mr. Moscovitz?
7. How did Gussie break her arm?
8. How do the girls who work at the shirtwaist factory spend their time and money?
9. How did Rose escape the fire?
10. What happened to Gussie and Maureen?

Discussion Questions

Discuss the following questions with a small group or the entire class.

1. Was Rose's family treated fairly at the Ellis Island center where they entered the United States? Give your reasons.
2. Why does Patrick's family resent helping Rose's family?
3. Why do Patrick's daughters think they are better than Rose's family?
4. Why did Ma let Rose and Maureen stay in America?
5. Why did Ma want to go back to Ireland?
6. Why did Mr. Garoff let Rose rent a room?
7. How does Rose get her pay from Mr. Moscovitz?
8. Why do Maureen and Rose fight?
9. Why is Gussie so involved in the union?
10. What happened during the fire at the factory that led to more deaths?
11. Who was responsible for Gussie's death? Give your reasons.
12. What did you learn from reading this book?

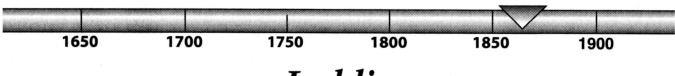

1650	1700	1750	1800	1850	1900

Lyddie

Lyddie by Katherine Paterson is the story of a country girl from Vermont who becomes a mill girl working in one of the Massachusetts textile factories during the 1840s. This book of historical fiction gives insight into the hopes and heartaches of the young women who were trying to improve their lives despite the harsh working conditions.

Comprehension Questions

Read the book *Lyddie*. Then answer the following questions on a separate sheet of paper.

1. Why did Lyddie and Charlie have to leave the farm?
2. Why was Lyddie distrustful of Quakers at first?
3. Why did Triphena like Lyddie?
4. To whom did Lyddie loan the 25 dollars?
5. What goal did Betsy have?
6. What did a *doffer* like Rachel do?
7. How much money did Lyddie have saved when she was discharged?
8. How did Lyddie protect Brigid from Mr. Marsden after she was fired?
9. What is Lyddie going to do in Ohio?
10. What did Luke want Lyddie to do?

Discussion Questions

Discuss the following questions with a small group or the entire class.

1. Why does Lyddie become the leader of the family when they live on the farm?
2. How does Lyddie change over time?
3. Did Lyddie make good choices in deciding to be a mill girl? Explain your answer.
4. Which mill girl was the most kind to Lyddie? Explain.
5. Should Lyddie have trusted Ezekial Abernathy, the runaway slave? Explain your answer.
6. Why was the book *Oliver Twist* so important to Lyddie?
7. Should Lyddie have joined and supported the union? Give your reasons.
8. Why did Lyddie's attitude toward Brigid change?
9. Why was Lyddie really discharged from her job?
10. How did Lyddie become like Diana?

Extension

Read *Oliver Twist* by Charles Dickens. Then write an essay explaining why the story would have appealed to Lyddie and Betsy.

1650 1700 1750 1800 1850 1900

Diaries

The fictionalized diaries listed on this page are based on the lives of real people who worked in the mills and factories of the industrial age. They reflect the experiences of immigrant girls and their families as they adjusted to life and culture in America. The authors are skilled writers as well as historians.

Fictional Diaries

Bartoletti, Susan Campbell. *A Coal Miner's Bride: The Diary of Anetka Kaminska.* Scholastic, 2000. (The story of a Polish immigrant girl who comes to America in an arranged marriage to an immigrant Pennsylvania coal miner)

Denenberg, Barry. *So Far from Home: The Diary of Mary Driscoll, an Irish Mill Girl.* Scholastic, 1997. (Diary of a girl forced by the Irish potato famine to immigrate to America)

Lasky, Kathryn. *Hope in My Heart: Sofia's Immigrant Diary, Book One.* Scholastic, 2003. (An excellent book in the My America series which details the life of an Italian immigrant family at the turn of the 20th century)

Lasky, Kathryn. *Home At Last: Sofia's Immigrant Diary, Book Two.* Scholastic, 2003. (The second book in the My America series about an Italian immigrant girl at the turn of the 20th century)

Lasky, Kathryn. *Dreams in the Golden Country: The Diary of Zipporah Feldman, a Jewish Immigrant Girl.* Scholastic, 1998. (Diary of an immigrant girl struggling with school, family, and life in America)

Assignment

Read one of the diaries listed above or another one set during the Industrial Revolution. Complete the Diary Evaluation on page 32. Then share what you learned with the class.

Extension

Use the information you have learned to write a letter to a friend or relative in another country who is planning to come to the United States to work. Describe the living and working conditions here, and give them advice they will need to cope with life in America.

Dear _____,

_____

_____

_____

_____

Sincerely yours,

_____

©Teacher Created Resources, Inc.

#3220 Industrial Revolution

Diary Evaluation

Title of diary: _____

Writer's Personal Data

Name: _____ Age: _____ Nationality: _____

Character traits (shy, fearful, proud, humble): _____

_____

Hopes and desires: _____

_____

Setting and Situation

Time and place: _____

Circumstances (job, living conditions): _____

_____

Dangers faced: _____

_____

Problems/conflicts: _____

_____

Important Characters in the Diary

Family: _____

_____

Friends/Neighbors: _____

_____

Others: _____

_____

Describe two interesting events.

   1. _____

      _____

   2. _____

      _____

Describe two sad events.

   1. _____

      _____

   2. _____

      _____

Impressions (Describe your impressions of the diary and the diarist.) _____

_____

_____

Readers' Theater Notes

Readers' Theater is drama that does not require costumes, props, stage, or memorization. It is done in the classroom by groups of students who become the cast of the dramatic reading.

Staging

Place four or five stools, chairs, or desks in a semicircle at the front of the classroom or in a separate staging area. Generally no costumes are used in this type of dramatization, but students dressed in similar clothing or colors can add a nice effect. Props are unnecessary but can be used.

Scripting

Each member of the group should have a clearly marked script. Performers should practice several times before presenting the play to the class.

Performing

Performers should enter the classroom quietly and seriously. They should sit silently without moving, and the first reader should begin. The other readers should focus on whoever is reading, except when they are performing.

Assignment

Choose one of the readers' theater scripts in this book: Triangle Terror (pages 34 and 35) or Child's Work (pages 36 and 37). Work with a group to prepare for the performance, and share your interpretation of the script with the class.

Extension

Write your own readers' theater script based on one of the events listed below or another topic related to the Industrial Revolution. Practice your script with a group of classmates, and then perform it for the rest of the class.

- the life of a child working in a factory or coal mine
- the challenge of steelworkers, coal miners, or factory workers trying to start a union
- an entire family working in a cannery or mill
- a family's struggles as migrant farm workers (Read *Esperanza Rising* by Pam Munoz Ryan.)
- the life of a new immigrant in the United States

Readers' Theater: Triangle Terror

This script tells about mill girls who worked at the Triangle Shirtwaist Factory in New York City, where a fire in March 1911 killed 146 workers. There are four speakers.

Narrator: In the early twentieth century, many young girls were employed in textile mills. Nell has newly arrived in the United States from Ireland, Clara is a Russian immigrant, and Hannah is a Jewish immigrant from Poland. All are mill girls working at the Triangle Shirtwaist Factory in New York City in 1911.

Nell: I hate those locked doors on each floor. I feel like I'm trapped in a prison. What do they think we're going to do—run away? We're eight floors up. There's no place to go.

Clara: They're so afraid we'll sneak in two minutes late. What's the difference? They dock our pay for any lost time, even if we're sick or hurt.

Hannah: They lock the doors to make sure we don't just walk out some day in one angry group. They fear our strength.

Nell: I hate the noise, too. The loud, screeching sound of all these machines can drive you insane. It makes my head hurt.

Clara: This factory reminds me of Russia with the police and soldiers constantly checking your papers and insulting you.

Nell: The women bosses here are always inspecting our clothes when we leave to make sure we don't steal a few inches of ribbon or a scrap of cloth. They treat us like common thieves.

Hannah: It's humiliating. We'd be a lot better off if we could get every working girl here to join the union and fight for our rights together.

Nell: It won't work. There are thousands of other girls who'd be happy to have our jobs. We don't make much money here, but we're not starving or doing piecework sewing just to survive.

Hannah: But we're slaves here—factory slaves. We don't have any power to get better pay, work fewer hours, or stay home when we're sick. Look at poor Agnes over there. She's had that cough for weeks, and it's getting worse. She got it from all of the dust and lint in the air here.

Clara: The windows aren't even open to provide ventilation. Agnes can't stay home or see a doctor because they'd fire her for missing work. She's the sole support of her crippled mother, but she could die from tuberculosis or some other disease. She's getting thinner and weaker every day.

Readers' Theater: Triangle Terror *(cont.)*

Nell: Lots of the girls have hacking coughs, but we've no choice. They fired Elizabeth when she lost three fingers in the machine she worked on. Since she couldn't work, she was no use to them anymore. What can we do?

Clara: I smell something burning. Somebody's machine must be overheating.

Hannah: Look, there's smoke!

Nell: That's a lot of smoke. That's no damaged machine. I think it's coming from the pile of waste fabric. Oh Lord, look at the blaze! The building's on fire!

Clara: Lenora's on fire! Help me smother the flames!

Narrator: The girls rush to gather cloth and smother the flames on Lenora's dress and they see that piles of cloth are spurting flame. The roar of the fire drowns out the sound of the other machines and dozens of girls are suddenly screaming and running toward the doors. The building is in pandemonium.

Nell: The doors are locked! Find a foreman! Get a key!

Clara: Smash the door! We have to get out! We'll be burned alive!

Hannah: The doors won't break! Check the others!

Narrator: Girls push against the doors in desperation and die crushed and suffocated by the smoke. The three friends can see flames spreading over the entire floor. Machines and cloth, walls and ceilings are all on fire. The thick smoke is choking and blinding them. Girls are collapsing. Many are now on fire.

Hannah: The doors are blocked. We can't get out that way. We've no choice but to jump through the windows.

Nell: We'll be cut to pieces, and it's eight floors to the ground. We'll die for sure!

Hannah: Probably, but anything's better than fire. Help me smash this window. Agnes and Harriet just jumped.

Clara: I'm burning! Help me!

Hannah: Nell, grab Clara! Hang on now, girls! Jump!

Narrator: The firemen's nets on the street broke, and the girls fell to their deaths. Of the 500 workers in the factory, 146 died either from the fire or jumped to their deaths. The Triangle Shirtwaist Fire on March 25, 1911, was a tragedy which awakened the nation to the dangers of factory life. It would be more than 25 years, however, before tough, stringent laws would be passed to prevent future catastrophes like this one.

1650   1700   1750   1800   1850   1900

Readers' Theater: Child's Work

In this script three children who worked at different jobs in 1911 are interviewed. There are five speakers.

Narrator: Welcome to the Living History Channel and our continuing series *A Look at America's Past* hosted by Jennifer Sloan. Each week she takes us back in time to a moment in American history that gives us a glimpse of life during that period.

Jennifer: Good evening, everyone. Tonight we will travel back to 1911, rewind the reels of history, and meet a group of children. These children are hard at work in our nation's mills, canneries, factories, mines, and farms. Our first guest is Dennis McKee, a young coal breaker in a West Virginia mine. Dennis, how long have you been working at this coal company?

Dennis: Well, Ma'am, I been working here about two years now.

Jennifer: How old are you?

Dennis: I'm 12, but I told 'em I was 14 cause the law says you gotta be 14. The foremen knew but don't really care anyhow. Most of us boys start work here when we're about 10. If inspectors come around, they just hide us for a couple hours, but then they also dock our pay. That don't seem fair though.

Jennifer: What do you do at the mine, Dennis?

Dennis: I'm a coal breaker. I sit in a little box with coal moving under me and pull out pieces of rock and other stuff that ain't coal. You gotta be real careful though. Two of my friends got caught last month and was carried down the chute and smothered to death. I lost two fingers myself a while back.

Jennifer: Our next guest is Molly Jackson who works in a Georgia textile mill as a spinner. How old are you, Molly, and what is your job?

Molly: I'm almost nine. I been working here every day since I was about seven—cept on Sundays, of course. Me 'n the other girls start work directly at six in the morning. We work 12-hour shifts. You can't be even a minute late or they docks your pay an hour. We spinners go up and down the aisles between the spinning machines and brush the lint off the machines.

Jennifer: Is it always this dusty in the mill?

Readers' Theater: Child's Work *(cont.)*

Molly: All this dust in the air is mostly just tiny bits of cloth. We can't let it get on the machines, or they'll clog up and break down. The thread on the bobbins sometimes breaks so we also have to tie the broken ends together so the machines don't stop. Girls is better at that cause our fingers is smaller and faster. There ain't no time to rest.

Boys are mostly doffers. They replace the spools of thread on the machines. That's tricky work. My younger brother caught his foot in a machine and busted it up bad. He's still working though.

Jennifer: Have you ever been to school, Molly?

Molly: I'd like to go to school, but it ain't likely. Nobody in my family can read or do sums. We all work once we can walk. Even though I only earn a few cents a day, we needs the money to eat and pay the rent on the shack that's our home.

Jennifer: Have you been to a doctor for your cough?

Molly: Everybody in the mill has a cough. All of us spinners gets one after being here a while. Some kids die from it, but most of us is luckier. Can't afford no doctor.

Jennifer: Our third guest is Jacob Caldwell. He is an oyster shucker in a Mississippi cannery. Jacob, how old are you and what kind of work do you do?

Jacob: I'm six now, but I been workin' with my parents since I was four. It took a while to learn how to crack open them oysters and shuck out the meat. I was pretty quick to learn how to use the shuckin' knife, but if you ain't extra careful, you'll slice off a finger or two like my brother did.

Jennifer: Your hands are scarred and bleeding. Wouldn't you rather be in school?

Jacob: Can't afford to go to school. We need the money to eat. They pay five cents for a pail of shucked oysters, and I make about 10 or 15 cents on a good day. The shells are sharp and cut your hands, but they scar over and harden. Shrimp are worse to shuck cause the acid eats the skin off your fingers and make holes in your clothes and boots. I don't specially like startin' work at three in the morning either.

Jennifer: Well, that wraps up our show today. I want to thank my three guests for joining us and telling us about their lives.

Narrator: Today you met three young children who worked in the United States in 1911. They were among the tens of thousands of children who had to work to help their families survive. They could not go to school, had very little time for play, and many died early from disease, accidents, and lack of proper food. It was a national tragedy. Thank you for joining us on *A Look at America's Past.*

Teacher Lesson Plans for Social Studies and Science

Time Line

Objectives: Students will learn to derive information from a time line and do research to add additional information to a time line.

Materials: copies of Time Line of the Industrial Revolution (page 39); research resources including books, encyclopedias, texts, atlases, almanacs, and Internet sites

Procedure

1. Collect available resources so that students have reference materials in which to find information.
2. Review the concept of a time line, using events from the current school year as an example.
3. Reproduce and distribute Time Line of the Industrial Revolution. Review the various events listed on the time line.
4. Instruct students to place additional dates on the time line as described in the assignment. Allow them to share the event they illustrated. Display these illustrations in chronological order on a classroom wall or bulletin board.

Assessment: Assess students' ability to research information. Verify the accuracy of the events and dates that students add to the time line.

Science Inventions and Projects

Objectives: Students will conduct research about important inventions, learn how to make an electromagnet, and perform experiments using the electromagnet.

Materials: copies of Revolutionary Inventions (page 40); reference materials including encyclopedias, textbooks, almanacs, and Internet sites; copies of Electromagnets (pages 41– 43); science materials listed on pages 41– 43 including sandpaper or scissors, insulated bell wire, metal bolt or nails, C or D cell batteries, strong rubber bands, small paper clips, various metal and other objects such as a pencil, pen, ruler, staples, penny, large paper clip, and dime, iron magnets with the north and south poles labeled

Procedure

1. Collect available resources so that students have reference materials in which to find information.
2. Reproduce and distribute the Revolutionary Inventions (page 40) activity sheet. Review the directions and how to use reference materials to find the date, use, and importance of each invention. Have students work independently or with a partner.
3. Collect the materials listed on each page before assigning each science project.
4. Reproduce and distribute the Electromagnets (pages 41– 43) experiments one page at a time or as a packet.
5. Review the directions for making each project and distribute the necessary materials. Allow students to demonstrate their completed models.

Assessment: Correct the Revolutionary Inventions work sheet together. For the science projects, have students share their electromagnet models with the class and discuss their results.

Time Line of the Industrial Revolution

1712 – Thomas Newcomen invents the first efficient steam engine.

1733 – John Kay invents the flying shuttle.

1764 – James Hargreaves invents the spinning jenny.

1769 – James Watt creates a practical steam engine.

– Richard Arkwright invents the spinning frame.

1790 – Samuel Slater opens a mill in Rhode Island.

1793 – Eli Whitney invents the cotton gin.

1807 – Robert Fulton builds the first successful steamboat.

1814 – First steam-powered textile mill opens in Massachusetts.

1825 – The Erie Canal is completed.

1830 – The first American locomotive, the *Tom Thumb,* is built.

1844 – Samuel Morse sends the first telegraph message between two cities.

1845 – Clock making becomes a factory business.

1846 – Elias Howe invents the first sewing machine.

1856 – Bessemer creates a better method of making steel.

1859 – The first oil well in America is drilled in Pennsylvania.

1866 – The National Labor Union is organized.

1867 – The typewriter is invented.

1869 – The first American transcontinental railroad is completed.

1870 – John D. Rockefeller creates the Standard Oil Corporation.

1872 – Andrew Carnegie opens a steel plant in Pittsburgh .

1876 – Alexander G. Bell receives a patent for the telephone.

1877 – Violent railroad strikes come as a result of pay cuts.

1879 – Thomas Edison invents the incandescent light bulb.

1882 – The Standard Oil Company becomes the first trust in America.

1886 – A nationwide strike led to shootings in Chicago's Haymarket Square.

1892 – A strike in Homestead, Pennsylvania, pits workers against strike breakers at the Carnegie steel plant.

1894 – The Pullman railroad workers strike is another setback for labor.

1908 – Ford Motor Company introduces the Model T, the first mass-produced car.

1911 – The Triangle Shirtwaist Factory fire kills 146 women.

1913 – Henry Ford introduces the use of conveyor belts in his automobile factory.

1929 – The stock market crash brings on the Great Depression.

1932 – The New Deal begins and efforts are made to curb child labor and help labor unions.

1938 – Fair Labor Standards Act sets a minimum wage, a 40-hour work week, and outlaws child labor.

Assignment

List at least 10 events in American history to add to the above time line. These could include wars, inventions, presidential elections, natural disasters, cultural fads, or sporting events. Then choose one of these events to illustrate, color, and label on a separate sheet of paper. Be sure to include the date.

| 1650 | 1700 | 1750 | 1800 | 1850 | 1900 |

Revolutionary Inventions

Many inventions helped bring about the Industrial Revolution. These inventions made possible the growth of factories, the transportation of raw materials and finished products, and the rapid communications between buyers and sellers.

Assignment

Find the year each of the following was invented. Describe the use and importance of each invention. Use encyclopedias, textbooks, almanacs, and the Internet.

Invention	Date	Use/Importance
1. Cotton gin	_____	_____
2. Electric motor	_____	_____
3. Internal combustion engine	_____	_____
4. Railroad locomotive	_____	_____
5. Sewing machine	_____	_____
6. Spinning jenny	_____	_____
7. Steam engine	_____	_____
8. Steamboat	_____	_____
9. Telegraph	_____	_____
10. Telephone	_____	_____

Electromagnets

The Industrial Revolution was driven by inventions which completely transformed transportation, communication, sources of power, and the production of goods. The invention of the electromagnet led to the telegraph, electric motors, the separation of ores, and many other uses.

Make an Electromagnet

Materials: sandpaper or scissors; 12 to 18 inches (30 to 46 cm) of thin, insulated bell wire; metal bolt or nail; C or D cell battery; strong rubber band; small paper clips; various metal and other objects such as a pencil, pen, ruler, staples, penny, large paper clip, dime, etc.

Procedure

1. Use sandpaper or scissors to strip one inch (2.5 cm) of the insulation off each end of the wire.

2. Leaving 3 inches (8 cm) of wire at the one end, wrap the wire neatly around the bolt or nail. Leave 3 inches (8 cm) of wire hanging at the other end.

3. Touch one bare end of the wire to the positive pole of the battery and the other bare end to the negative pole of the battery. Use a strong rubber band to hold the wires in place against the poles.

Using the Electromagnet

Procedure

1. Hold the top of the bolt or nail near some small paper clips. How many paper clips does the magnet attract? _____

2. What other objects does the electromagnet attract? Try these or other objects. Put a checkmark if the item is magnetic.

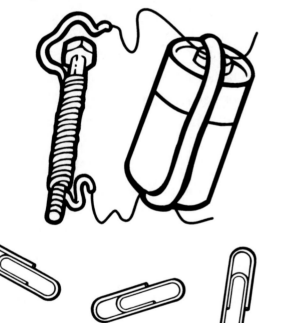

_____ pencil

_____ pen

_____ ruler

_____ staples

_____ penny

_____ large paper clip

_____ dime

_____ other (_____)

Electromagnets *(cont.)*

Using the Opposite End

Materials: electromagnet made on page 41; iron magnet with poles labeled N (north) and S (south); small paper clips

Procedure

1. Hold the other end of the bolt or nail near some small paper clips. How many paper clips does the magnet attract? _____

2. Can you pick up as many clips? _____

3. Can you pick up more clips? _____

Naming the Poles

Every magnet has two poles—a north pole and a south pole. You can identify the poles of an electromagnet by using an iron magnet with the poles labeled.

Materials: electromagnet made on page 41; iron magnet with poles labeled N (north) and S (south)

Procedure

1. Hold the iron magnet with the north pole next to one pole of your connected electromagnet.
   - If they attract each other, that electromagnetic pole is a south pole.
   - If they repel (push away) each other, that electromagnetic pole is a north pole.

2. Try the same thing with the other pole of the electromagnet.

Comparing Other Electromagnets

Materials: electromagnet made on page 41

Procedure

1. Hold the head of your electromagnet to the head of a friend's electromagnet. Do they attract or repel? _____

2. Hold the tail of your electromagnet to the tail of a friend's electromagnet. Do they attract or repel? _____

3. Hold the head of your electromagnet to the tail of a friend's electromagnet. Do they attract or repel? _____

Electromagnets *(cont.)*

Switching Poles

Materials: electromagnet made on page 41; iron magnet with poles labeled N (north) and S (south)

Procedure

1. Reverse the wires attached to the battery.

2. Use the iron magnet to find the north and south poles of the electromagnet. Describe what happened.

Comparing Strength

Materials: electromagnet made on page 41; small paper clips

Procedure

1. Work with a partner. Each student should hold his or her electromagnet $1\frac{1}{2}$ inches (4 cm) from the paper clips.

2. Count how many clips were attracted to each magnet.

   My magnet attracted _____ paper clips.

   My partner's magnet attracted _____ paper clips.

3. Each partner should then hold his or her electromagnet $\frac{3}{8}$ inch (1 centimeter) from the paper clips.
4. Count how many clips were attracted to each magnet.

   My magnet attracted _____ paper clips.

   My partner's magnet attracted _____ paper clips.

5. How far away can you hold the electromagnet and still attract paper clips?

More Power

Materials: electromagnet made on page 41; additional C or D cell battery; metal bolt or nail; additional thin, insulated bell wire; small paper clips

Procedure

1. Connect two batteries in a row with the positive pole of one battery touching the negative pole of the other.

2. Attach one wire to the positive pole of the first battery and the other bare end to the negative pole of the second battery. Can you pick up more paper clips? _____

3. Replace the wire on your nail or bolt with a longer piece of wire. Be sure to strip the ends and wind the wire carefully. Can you pick up more paper clips? _____

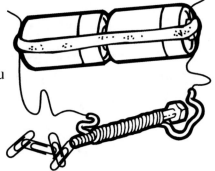

Culminating Activities

Relive the Industrial Revolution

Set aside a day to devote to activities related to your study of the Industrial Revolution.

Parent Help

Encourage parents or adult family members to help set up, monitor, and enjoy the activities. See if they have any special talents, interests, or hobbies that would be a match for specific centers.

Creating Centers

Set up centers that relate in some way to the Industrial Revolution, daily life in the 19th and early 20th centuries in America, or activities from this book. Centers should involve small groups of six or seven students doing an activity and/or making something they can display. The class is divided into groups with about six or seven students in each group. Each center should take about 20 minutes after which time students should rotate to the next activity. The following are suggestions for various centers. You may add others for which you have special expertise.

☐ **Organize a Union**

Have students use what they learned to organize a meeting where they discuss the length of the work day and work week, their pay, benefits for sick and injured workers, retirement, working conditions, and other grievances held by the workers. Some students could represent workers and others the business owners. Encourage students to debate the issues.

☐ **Perform Readers' Theater**

This center involves practicing for a readers' theater presentation. Students can use a script in this book or one they wrote and then present it to parents or other classes.

☐ **Make a Class Mural**

Provide a long piece of butcher paper and colored pencils, markers, poster paint, or other materials for students to create a class mural with images of the Industrial Revolution. Students can draw scenes of factory workers, inventions, child workers, labor strikes and clashes with business owners, and similar pictures. Each group of students can illustrate a separate section of the mural.

☐ **Become an Inventor**

Students can use modeling clay, craft sticks, construction paper, aluminum foil, paper clips, paper towel tubes, and other materials to create models of telegraphs, telephones, spinning jennies, locomotives, steamboats and other inventions of the era.

Annotated Bibliography

Fiction

Auch, Mary Jane. *Ashes of Roses.* Random House, 2002. (Intriguing story of an immigrant Irish girl caught in the politics and fire at the Triangle Shirtwaist Factory in 1911)

Denenberg, Barry. *So Far from Home: The Diary of Mary Driscoll, an Irish Mill Girl.* Scholastic, 1997. (Fictional diary of a girl forced by the Irish potato famine to immigrate to America)

Lasky, Kathryn. *Dreams in the Golden Country: The Diary of Zipporah Feldman, a Jewish Immigrant Girl.* Scholastic, 1998. (Fictional diary of an immigrant girl struggling with school, family, and life)

Paterson, Katherine. *Lyddie.* Scholastic, 1991. (Story of a mill girl in the early 1800s)

Nonfiction

Clare, John D. (Ed). *Industrial Revolution.* Harcourt, 1994. (Detailed report of the growth of industrialization, its effects on people's lives, and its impact on the world)

Collier, Christopher and James Lincoln Collier. *The Rise of Industry 1860–1900.* Cavendish, 2000. (Clear, cogent overview of the rise of America as an industrial giant and the problems created for workers and citizens)

Collins, Mary. *The Industrial Revolution.* Children's Press, 2000. (Easy-to-read review of industrialization in England and the United States)

Freedman, Russell. *Kids at Work: Lewis Hine and the Crusade Against Child Labor.* Clarion, 1994. (History of children working in the factories and mines of America and the schoolteacher/photographer who led the crusade against child labor)

Freedman, Russell. *Immigrant Kids.* Scholastic, 1992. (A brief overview of the lives of immigrant children in America during the age of industrialization)

Gourley, Catherine. *Good Girl Work.* Millbrook, 1999. (History of girl workers from the early 1800s to the Triangle Shirtwaist Factory fire in 1911)

Grant, R.G. *The Great Depression.* Barrons, 2002. (An account of the Great Depression written for middle-grade students)

McCormick, Anita Louise. *The Industrial Revolution in American History.* Enslow, 1998. (Account of the rise of industrialization in England and its rapid progress through America in the 19th and 20th centuries)

Saller, Carol. *Working Children.* Carolrhoda, 1998. (Exceptional illustrations and vignettes of child labor during the 19th and early 20th centuries)

Wroble, Lisa A. *Kids During the Industrial Revolution.* Rosen, 1999. (Brief account of the effects of the Industrial Revolution on the lives of children)

Glossary

bobbin—spool holding thread or yarn

canal—a man-made waterway connecting natural waterways

capital—investment money for business

coal—a black mineral burned for fuel

coke—coal which has been heated and is used to make iron

competition—rivalry in business

corporation—a large business

factory—a building where manufacturing of goods is done

freight—merchandise or goods being transported

immigration—to come to a different country to live

interchangeable parts—products made so that each part is exactly the same size

loom—a machine used to weave wool

manufacture—to make a product by hand or by machine

merger—two or more companies combining

mill—a small factory using running water for power

monopoly—control of a product or industry by one company or person

outsource—send work (goods or services) outside of a company, sometimes to another country

patent—legal protection for an inventor

profit—the money made by a business after all of the expenses and taxes are paid

raw material—wood, leather, cloth or other basic resources made into finished products

robber barons—businessmen who accumulated huge personal fortunes, generally through unfair business practices

spinning wheel—a foot-powered device used to make thread

steamboat—a paddleboat powered by a steam engine

steam engine—engine used to power machines in factories

steel—a strong metal made from iron and carbon

strike—a work stoppage by employees to get better pay, benefits, or working conditions

survival of the fittest—the idea that only the strongest will survive

telegraph—a machine which uses electric signals to send messages

tenement—run-down housing where poor families live

textile—cloth

transportation—moving goods or people from one place to another

trusts—giant, powerful businesses which control an industry

union—a group of workers who try to get better wages and working conditions

wages—money paid to a person for his or her work

Answer Key

Page 20
1. a
2. c
3. d
4. b
5. c
6. d
7. a
8. d
9. b
10. d

Page 21
1. d
2. d
3. b
4. a
5. a
6. b
7. d
8. c
9. c
10. d

Page 22
1. c
2. d
3. c
4. d
5. b
6. a
7. a
8. d
9. c
10. d

Page 23
1. b
2. a
3. a
4. b
5. c
6. d
7. b
8. d
9. a
10. a

Page 24
1. c
2. b
3. a
4. d
5. a
6. d
7. d
8. d
9. b
10. b

Page 27
1. k
2. l
3. f
4. g
5. j
6. h
7. b
8. c
9. e
10. i
11. a
12. d
13. loom
14. capital
15. monopoly

16. mill
17. steam engine
18. union
19. competition
20. tenement

Page 29
Comprehension Questions
1. Ireland
2. He had trachoma, an eye disease.
3. using a buttonhook to lift the eyelid
4. new immigrants
5. making paper flowers
6. the man who hired Rose to make flowers
7. A policeman broke it during a strike.
8. at the nickelodeon and on clothes
9. She slid down the elevator cable.
10. Maureen lived, but Gussie died.

Discussion Questions
1. Answers may vary.
2. They think they are better or higher class than Rose's family.
3. They have money and can go to school.
4. Ma gave in to Rose's request, and Maureen insisted on staying, too.
5. Ma missed Ireland and her husband and child and did not like New York.
6. He knew she needed the room and felt sorry for her.

Answer Key *(cont.)*

Page 29 *(cont.)*

7. Gussie helps her, and they make a scene.
8. Maureen wants to work, and Rose wants her to go to school.
9. Gussie believes it is the only hope for workers.
10. The doors were locked, and the girls panicked.
11. Answers may include the owners, the foremen, her own courage.
12. Answers may include the history of unions, factory labor, and industrialization.

Page 30

Comprehension Questions

1. Their mother rented the farm to others.
2. She had been taught to dislike them.
3. Lyddie worked hard and was quiet.
4. Ezekial Abernathy, the runaway slave
5. to go to college
6. keep the lint off machines and replace thread
7. $243.87
8. Lyddie threatened to tell Mr. Marsden's wife of his behavior.
9. go to college
10. marry him

Discussion Questions

1. Lyddie has the strength and determination.

2. She grows stronger, more careful, and determined to better herself.
3. Yes, it was her best choice for a job.
4. Answers will vary.
5. Yes, because he needed the help, and he paid her back the money.
6. She learned to read from the book, and she could relate to the story.
7. Answers may vary.
8. She felt sorry for Brigid and remembered Diana's help.
9. Lyddie angered Mr. Marsden by protecting Brigid.
10. She cared for others.

Page 40

(**Note:** Answers may vary depending upon the sources used.)

1. Cotton gin, 1793, made cotton production and textile plants profitable
2. Electric motor, 1873, provided a cheap, powerful source of energy
3. Internal combustion engine, 1860, made possible the automobile which fueled the second Industrial Revolution
4. Railroad locomotive, 1804, greatly increased the amount of material that could be moved cheaply

5. Sewing machine, 1846, greatly increased the speed of clothes production
6. Spinning jenny, about 1764, could spin eight threads rather than just one
7. Steam engine, 1712, provided power for factories and railroads
8. Steamboat, 1787, greatly improved transportation speeds
9. Telegraph, 1837, greatly speeded up communication between cities
10. Telephone, 1876, speeded up communication for businessmen and consumers